CAM.

MUSIC FROM THE MOTION PICTURE

Pine trees ©istockphoto.com/Terrance Emerson
Male silhouettes ©istockphoto.com/Joshua Blake
Female silhouette, right ©123rf.com/Kirsty Pargeter
Female silhouette, left ©123rf.com/Galina Barskaya

Alfred Publishing Co., Inc.
16320 Roscoe Blvd., Suite 100
P.O. Box 10003
Van Nuys, CA 91410-0003
alfred.com

ISBN-10: 1-5762-3346-4
ISBN-13: 978-0-7390-4783-5

CONTENTS

HOW SHALL I SEE YOU THROUGH MY TEARS 3

CENTURY PLANT 9

HERE'S WHERE I STAND 17

I SING FOR YOU 26

THE WANT OF A NAIL 30

WILD HORSES 39

THE LADIES WHO LUNCH 42

TURKEY LURKEY TIME 48

SKYWAY 57

THE SIZE OF A COW 61

ON/OFF 68

RIGHT ON BE FREE 72

I BELIEVE IN US 80

ROUND ARE WAY 86

HOW SHALL I SEE YOU THROUGH MY TEARS

Words and Music by
ROBERT TELSON and LEE BREUER

*Vocals written at pitch.

Verse 2:
Father, sister, the gods have spoken,
I bring a promise, a holy vow.
A world that casts you down forgives you,
And those who blame you sing your praises now.
So can you tell me...
(To Chorus:)

CENTURY PLANT

Words and Music by
VICTORIA ANN WILLIAMS

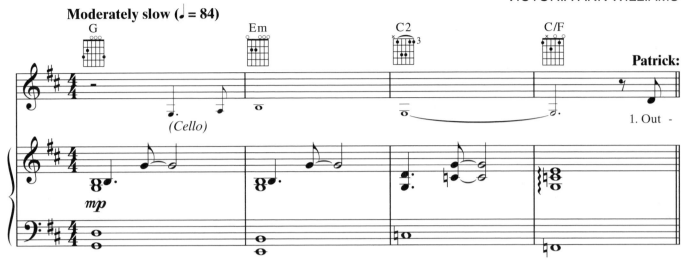

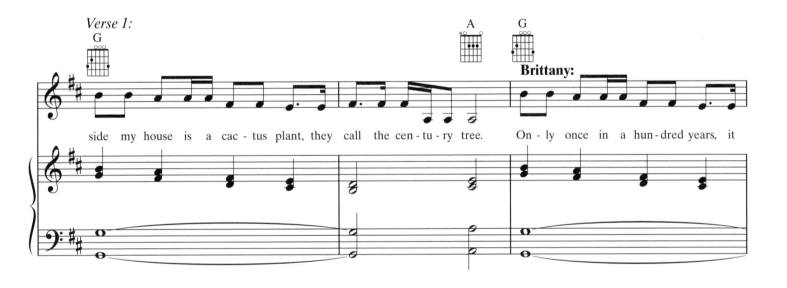

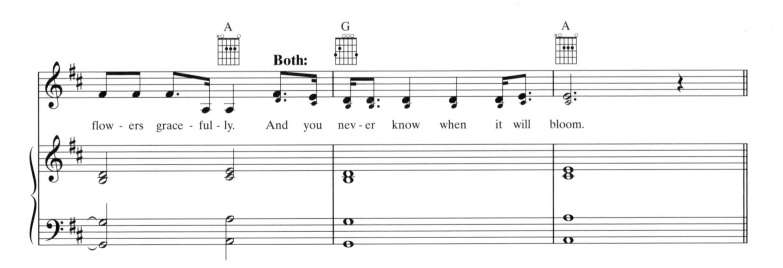

HERE'S WHERE I STAND

Lyrics by
LYNN AHRENS

Music by
MICHAEL GORE

Here in the dark, I stand be-fore you, know-ing this is my chance to show you my___ heart. This is the___ start, this is the___

18

I SING FOR YOU

Lyrics by
LYNN AHRENS

Music by
MICHAEL GORE

THE WANT OF A NAIL

Words and Music by
TODD RUNDGREN

*Vocals written at pitch.

The Want of a Nail - 9 - 1
28177

Verse 2:
Michael: For the want of a rider, the message was lost.
Dee: For the want of a message, the battle was lost.
Michael: For the want of a battle, the war was lost.
Dee: For the want of a war, the kingdom was lost.
(To Chorus:)

WILD HORSES

Words and Music by
MICK JAGGER and KEITH RICHARDS

THE LADIES WHO LUNCH

(from "Company")

Music and Lyrics by
STEPHEN SONDHEIM

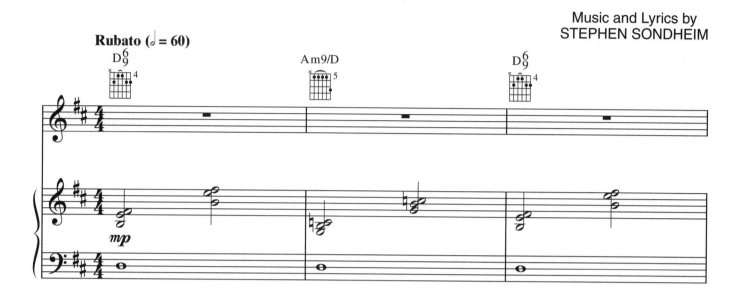

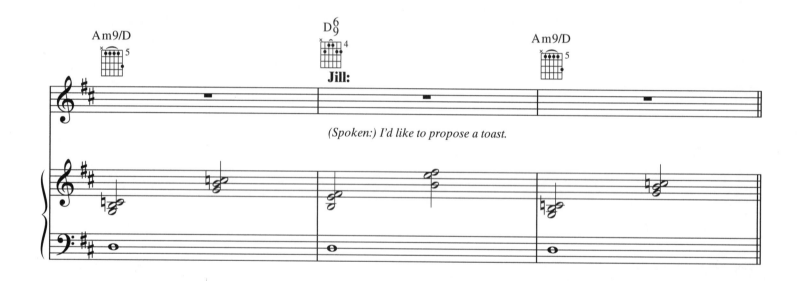

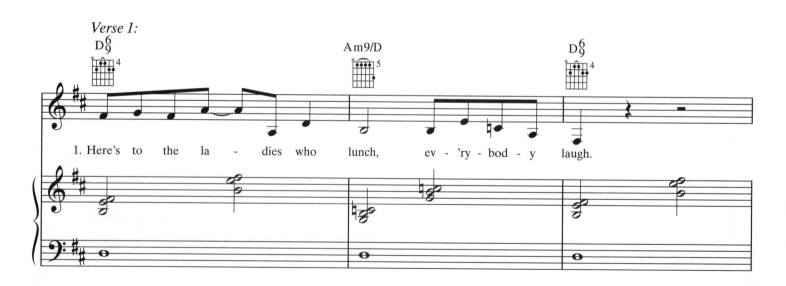

Verse 4:

Fritzi: 4. So, here's to the girls___ on the go,___ ev - 'ry - bod - y tries.

Look in - to their eyes and you'll see___ what they know:___ Ev - 'ry - bod - y dies.___ A toast to that in - vin - ci - ble bunch,___ the di - no - saurs sur - viv - ing the crunch.___

TURKEY LURKEY TIME

Words and Music by
BURT BACHARACH and HAL DAVID

Jill, Dequina, Tracy, & Company:

1. It's tur-key lur-key time. Tom tur-key ran a - way, but he just came
2. It's goo-sey Lu-cy time. She was a gad-a-bout, but she's back a -

home.___ It's tur-key lur-key time. He's real-ly home to
gain.___ It's goo-sey Lu-cy time. Her time is run-ning

stay, nev-er one to roam.___ }
out, and we all know when.___ } Let's make a wish, and may

SKYWAY

Words and Music by
PAUL WESTERBERG

Verse 2:
...to take the skyway.
It don't move at all like a subway.
It's got bums when it's cold like any other place.
It's warm up inside.
Sittin' down and waitin' for a ride
Beneath the skyway.

THE SIZE OF A COW

Words and Music by
MALCOLM TREECE, MARTIN GILKS,
MILES HUNT, ROBERT JONES,
MARTIN BELL and PAUL CLIFFORD

Chorus:

64

The Size of a Cow - 7 - 4
28177

Verse 2:
You know it would be strange to live life in a cage,
And only believe the things you see that are written on the page.
How easy would it be, home in time for tea,
And stop feeling like a sailboat rocking on the sea.
(To Pre-chorus:)

ON/OFF

Words and Music by
GARY LIGHTBODY, MARK McCLELLAND
and JONATHAN QUINN

Moderately slow ($\quarternote = 104$)

(Drums)

Verse:

(Play 2nd time, let ring)

1. I could-n't be-lieve___ what I was see - ing.___
2. Run-ning a - way___ seemed like the eas - y___

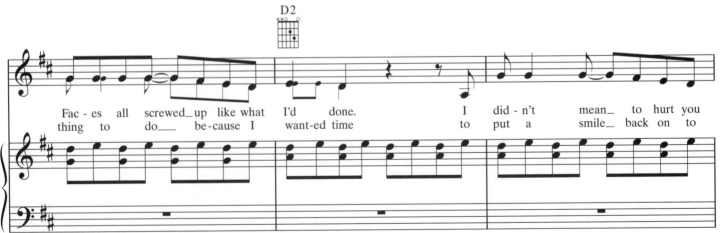

Fac - es all screwed_up like what I'd done.   I did - n't mean_ to hurt you
thing to do__ be-cause I want-ed time   to put a smile_ back on to

RIGHT ON BE FREE

Words and Music by
CHUCK GRIFFIN

Moderate driving funk (♩ = 126)

1. I wan-na go where the rough wind blows.___
2. See additional lyrics

Moth - er, moth - er, moth - er,   moth - er, save_____ your child._____

Organic solo:

C#m7

Repeat ad lib. and fade

Verse 2:
I want those clouds over my head.
(Over my head, over my head.)
I don't want no store bought bed, yeah.
(Store bought bed, store bought bed.)
I'm gonna live until I'm dead.
('Til I'm dead, 'til I'm dead.)
Mother, mother, mother, mother,
Save your child.
(To Chorus:)

I BELIEVE IN US

Words and Music by
JON LIND, WENDY WALDMAN
and PHIL GALDSTON

Chorus 3:

ROUND ARE WAY

Words and Music by
NOEL GALLAGHER